Heritage Conservation in America: An Introduction

This publication was written as a basic introduction to American preservation for an international audience. It details the preservation movement's origins and development, the main public, private and non-profit entities, financial and policy incentives, preservation's connection with sustainable development and a comparison with the British model. It is one of a series of publications produced by Heritage Strategies International.

Heritage Strategies International is a Washington DC-based consulting firm offering services on the economic evaluation of historic resources and integrating heritage buildings into economic development strategies. We provide professional, high quality education, information, and technical assistance internationally to clients seeking to encourage the economically productive use of heritage resources. Our clients include local and national governments, international non-governmental organizations, international development banks and others.

Donovan Rypkema is President of Heritage Strategies International. He is the author of *The Economics of Historic Preservation: A Community Leader's Guide* and an adjunct professor in the Historic Preservation program at the University of Pennsylvania. Caroline Cheong, Director of Research, holds a master's degree in historic preservation from the University of Pennsylvania and an undergraduate degree in anthropology from the University of Chicago. She recently held a one-year research appointment at the Getty Conservation Institute in Los Angeles.

Heritage Strategies International
1785 Massachusetts Avenue
Washington, DC 20036
+1 202 588 6258
info@hs-intl.com

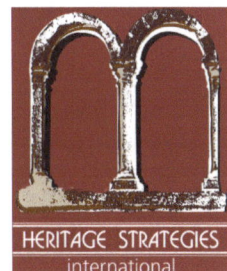

HERITAGE STRATEGIES
international

Contents

Introduction

The preservation of the historic built environment is a public policy priority in many countries. Historic buildings are seemingly always at risk. When economies are strong, historic buildings are often torn down for newer, larger structures. When economies are weak, heritage buildings are often lost through abandonment, lack of maintenance and demolition by neglect.

The historic preservation movement began in the United States a century and a half ago. Many of the philosophical and legal approaches to preservation in America were taken from countries in Western Europe. But over the last 150 years, American heritage conservation, or historic preservation as it is called in the United States, has evolved to respond to the particular American political and economic context.

Today historic preservation is a complex matrix of laws, incentives, policies and advocacy groups at the national, state and local level. There is active participation from the public, private and non-profit sectors. This network of interests spans geographical, political, social and economic perspectives.

More importantly, however, historic preservation has become a fundamental tool for strengthening American communities. It has proven to be an effective vehicle for a wide range of public goals including small business incubation, affordable housing, sustainable development, neighborhood stabilization, center city revitalization, job creation, promotion of the arts and culture, small town renewal, heritage tourism, economic development, and others.

For the most part America's historic buildings aren't fenced off and available only on public holidays. Rather they are part of the daily lives of Americans in every part of the country.

On the following pages is the story of American preservation, where it came from and how it has evolved. All three sectors of the economy and all three levels of government have important roles in historic preservation and we've tried to illustrate those roles through examples of laws, programs and organizations that make up the mosaic of preservation in America.

These pages are not intended to answer every question about how historic preservation works in the United States. Rather they are intended to offer an overview of the important ingredients of heritage conservation and provide the reader with online references where any particular element may be further explored.

There are still losses of historic buildings in the United States. But the historic preservation movement is no longer seen as an esoteric, aesthetically driven interest group holding country club fund raisers and occasionally standing in front of bulldozers. Far more often preservationists are at the table as valuable contributors in strengthening American communities large and small.

This is the story of American historic preservation and preservationists.

Brief History of Historic Preservation in America

The United States is a young nation. But there are heritage resources far older than the country itself. The Spanish colonial Palace of the Governors in Santa Fe, New Mexico was built in 1610, more than 150 years before the Declaration of Independence in 1776. There are numerous examples of both Spanish and English colonial buildings dating from the early 17th century.

But America's built heritage far predates the Europeans' arrival in the New World. Pueblo cliff dwellings are dated from the 6th to the 12th century. There is archeological evidence of habitation by aboriginal people hundreds of years before that.

Still, as compared to ancient structures in Africa, Asia and Europe, most of the inventory of historic assets in the United States is relatively young. But efforts to preserve the built history of the United States began 150 years ago.

The Beginning of Historic Preservation

It began with the single-handed efforts of Ann Pamela Cunningham. In 1853 Ms. Cunningham received a letter from her mother who had been traveling down the Potomac River by boat. The elder Cunningham wrote to her daughter:

Mt. Vernon, Virginia

It was a lovely moonlit night that we went down the Potomac. I went on deck as the bell tolled and we passed Mount Vernon. I was painfully distressed at the ruin and desolation of the home of Washington, and the thought passed through my mind: Why was it the women of his country did not try to keep it in repair, if the men could not do it?

Mount Vernon was the home of George Washington, first President of the United States and still referred to as the Father of his country. Her mother's lament about Mount Vernon became Ann Pamela Cunningham's call to action. In 1854 she formed the Mount Vernon Ladies' Association and by 1858 had managed to raise $200,000 in donations from around the country to purchase the Mount Vernon estate. Through this effort the historic preservation movement in America was born.

The "Voluntary Associations"

Frenchman Alexis de Tocqueville visited the United States in 1831 and returned home to write *Democracy in America*. Among the things he most admired about the new nation was the propensity of citizens to form "voluntary associations." In 1889 just such a "voluntary association" was formed – the Association for the Preservation of Virginia Antiquities. APVA was founded as a statewide, non-profit organization dedicated to preserving the built heritage important in the history of Virginia. This pattern of preservation advocacy and education by a statewide non-profit organization continues to this day.

The First Federal Actions

The enactment of laws for the protection of historic resources, however, didn't occur until early in the 20th century, first with the passage of the Federal Antiquities Act in 1906. The act was passed in part because of concern about plundering of Native American sites in the southwest United States.

But the law was largely confined to federal lands. It authorized the President to declare areas within federal ownership as National Monuments and prohibited the excavation, destruction or appropriation of antiquities on federal lands without a permit.

The Start of Historic Preservation Commissions

The *Vieux Carré* or French Quarter in New Orleans is a National Historic Landmark District and is one of America's most historic neighborhoods, with the earliest buildings dating to the 18th century. New Orleans also claims title to creating the first local historic district, having established the Vieux Carré Commission in 1925. There was one serious deficiency with the Commission, however; its role was only advisory with no powers of enforcement. That lesson was understood when the next local historic district was created. In 1931 the City of Charleston, South Carolina designated a 138-acre "Old and Historic District." As part of that ordinance a Board of Architectural Review (BAR) was established. While in its earliest years the formal power of the BAR was limited to reviewing demolition requests, it set the pattern for local preservation commissions as they exist today in the United States. In 1936 New Orleans recognized the limitations of its earlier commission and reformulated it to include enforcement provisions.

It is certainly no accident that the early actions of these two cities – New Orleans and Charleston – resulted in today their being among the best-loved US cities by Americans and visitors alike.

The Great Depression and HABS

In the 1930s the United States, like all Western countries, was faced with the Great Depression, with millions of its citizens unemployed. Although there were multiple responses by the federal government to address those needs, one in particular has had a lasting impact on historic preservation – the HABS program. HABS stands for the Historic American Buildings Survey. Included among the unemployed during the Depression were thousands of architects, photographers and draftsman. HABS was established within the National Park Service to make work for these professionals. Participants were sent across the country to document – through measured drawings, photographs and written reports – a sampling of American architecture. HABS is rightfully called the oldest federal government preservation program.

This archive of narrative and visual documents has become a treasure-house of materials for American preservationists. The HABS program still exists and has been supplemented by HAER – the Historic American Engineering Record – and HALS – the Historic American Landscape Survey. The HABS/HAER/HALS archive continues to grow and is being digitized for the use of preservationists generations into the future.

The National Trust for Historic Preservation

The end of World War II spurred a sense of confidence and leadership in the American people and in Congress. The country no longer felt "too young" to be concerned about its heritage. Thus Congress in 1949 created the National Trust for Historic Preservation. Although chartered by Congress, the National Trust is a non-profit organization and not part of the federal government. There is more discussion of the National Trust below.

Losses Lead to Legislation

The preservation movement in America is often catalyzed through the loss of an important or beloved building. Just such an event took place in New York City in 1963, with the demolition of the Pennsylvania

**Penn Station
New York, NY**

Railroad Station. This magnificent structure had been constructed in 1910 and was designed by one of America's foremost architectural firms, McKim, Mead and White. Although barely 50 years old at the time, Penn Station had provided the grand entry to Manhattan for millions of New Yorkers and visitors. Its loss spurred the creation of the New York City Landmarks Commission two years later.

But the loss of Penn Station also had a national impact. If one of the most important buildings in America's largest city could be lost to the bulldozer, weren't historic buildings at risk everywhere? That concern led, in part, to the passage of the National Historic Preservation Act in 1966. NHPA established the framework for federal policy toward historic preservation that remains today. NHPA is discussed below.

Non-Profits and Preservation Action

Under US law some non-profit organizations (NGOs) can receive donations from corporations and individuals, and the donor can take a tax deduction in the amount of the contribution. There is a catch, however. That type of non-profit organization cannot be involved in political activities. Other non-profit organizations can be politically active, but their funders cannot claim a tax deduction for their donations. The National Trust for Historic Preservation falls into the first category of organization and therefore cannot be directly involved in political activities. But preservation activists recognized that ultimately to be successful, there needed to be an organization that was willing and able to lobby members of Congress and the executive branch on behalf of historic preservation. In 1974 Preservation Action was founded. Preservation Action today is a national, grass roots political organization that seeks to make historic preservation a national policy priority.

The Bicentennial and Federal Tax Incentives

In the year 1976 the United States celebrated its bicentennial. This event triggered celebrations in virtually every city, town and village in America. As part of those celebrations individual citizens came to appreciate the history of their own community, and the buildings that were the physical manifestation of that history. It was in that year that the first federal tax incentives were passed to encourage private investment in historic buildings.

Subsequent changes in the tax law in 1978, 1981 and 1986 ultimately created the structure of investment incentives for historic buildings that exists today. These incentives are discussed below.

Bipartisan Support from First Ladies

In 1998 and in 2004 two First Ladies – Hillary Clinton and Laura Bush – gave new emphasis to historic preservation. Hillary Clinton was the founding chair of a program called *Save America's Treasures*, a public-private partnership that leverages federal appropriations with private sector donations. Laura Bush became the leading proponent of *Preserve America,* an initiative that, among other things, designated Preserve America communities, acknowledging towns and cities that have used their historic assets for economic development and community revitalization. The active involvement of these two First Ladies, from different political parties, demonstrates the bipartisan support that historic preservation usually commands in the United States. However, in 2010 the Obama administration discontinued these programs.

4

How the American Approach to Historic Preservation Differs from Other Countries

Each country has its own approach to historic preservation. In fact even the vocabulary can be different. In the United States the movement to identify, protect and enhance the historic built environment is called *historic preservation* rather than *heritage conservation* as it is in most of the rest of the world. Advocates in this movement are called *preservationists*. In the US *conservation* and *conservationists* are more commonly associated with the natural environment. When *conservation* is applied in the built heritage field, it generally refers to the physical conservation of materials, whereas *preservation* has a broader political, policy and social implication.

But beyond vocabulary, the philosophy, legal protections and roles can vary widely between countries. In Azerbaijan, for example, only the national government can own historic properties of national importance. There is no such restriction in the US where over half of the National Historic Landmarks are privately owned.

In some European countries there is a constitutional obligation placed on the government to protect the country's built heritage. There is no equivalent provision in the United States Constitution.

The US versus the British System

But to understand fundamental differences perhaps the comparison of the US and the British systems provides the clearest distinctions.

Although much of American preservation law and practice had the British experience as its basis, the two systems have evolved much differently. In Britain there are very strong protections for heritage property at the level of the national government for both publicly and privately owned properties. These protections come about largely though regulations on what can be done to historic buildings, and much heritage conservation is done directly by the public sector.

In the United States, by contrast, there is very little protection of heritage properties at the national level. Regulations that do exist are almost always at the local level. Owners of historic properties are often encouraged to appropriately treat heritage buildings through incentives rather than regulations. And by far most historic preservation is done by the private sector.

In a somewhat over-simplified fashion, then, it might be said that the differences between the systems are that the British system is top-down, regulation driven and public sector while the US system is bottom-up, incentive driven and private sector. It is not that one system is inherently better than the other. But the US system has evolved based on American concepts of local land use laws, property rights and federalism.

Federalism

Federalism is a form of government in which powers and responsibilities are shared among different levels of government. The United States was originally conceived as a federation of states – the original 13 colonies which declared independence from Great Britain. This concept of federalism has been, therefore, central to American government from the very beginning.

In the US there are three levels of government: the national government (also often referred to as the federal government), 50 state governments and thousands of units of local government. *Local government* usually refers to towns, cities, counties, and school districts.

The US Constitution spells out specific roles and responsibilities for the national government – foreign policy and national defense, for example. In principle, powers not explicitly granted to the national government are left to the states. This is sometimes referred to as the sovereignty of the states or states' rights.

Local governments, on the other hand, are generally limited in their powers to what is specifically delegated to them by state legislatures. While there is some variation among state laws, usually local government is authorized to have local police and fire departments, run the school system, build streets, and provide water and sewer systems and similar local services.

Local Government and Land Use Regulations

But importantly in relation to historic preservation, it is at the local level where land use laws are adopted. Land use laws include such things as building codes and zoning ordinances which specify public restrictions on what can be done with privately owned land. Laws for the protection of historic properties are part of the land use regulation authority granted by state legislatures to local governments.

The fundamental differences in the approach to historic preservation in the United States as compared Western Europe in large measure stems from this fundamental concept of federalism in the US governmental and legal system.

Role of the Public Sector

The role of the public sector in relation to historic preservation, although different than in Europe, is significant in the United States. It is the public sector that sets up the regulations by which historic properties are treated, but also provides many of the incentives that encourage private investment in heritage resources. Because governments at all levels are also significant owners of historic properties, they are also expected to teach by example the appropriate treatment of heritage buildings through their own stewardship and maintenance efforts.

But because of the principle of federalism, it is necessary to understand the decidedly different roles that each level of government has regarding heritage resources.

The Federal Government

At the federal level there are historic preservation responsibilities across departments. The federal government mandates stewardship for properties owned directly by the government and requires an analysis of any negative impact on historic properties as a result of the expenditure of federal funds. It does not, however, limit what individual property owners may do with their own heritage structures; that is left to state and primarily local governments.

National law requires that every department within the federal government have a Preservation Officer. The Preservation Officer has the responsibility of advising the Secretary of that department on that agency's preservation responsibilities and serves as a general "watchdog" over the department's activities that may affect historic properties.

While there is almost no regulation of privately owned historic properties at the national level, the federal government does provide a variety of incentives for historic preservation and has a number of grant funds that can be used for historic preservation activities.

Below are the key elements in historic preservation at the national government level.

The National Historic Preservation Act (NHPA)

Although some legislation affecting historic resources in the United States dates from early in the 20th century, the framework that exists today is largely that which was created in the National Historic Preservation Act of 1966. NHPA begins with the reasons such legislation was needed including, "the preservation of this irreplaceable heritage is in the public interest so that its vital legacy of cultural, educational, aesthetic, inspirational, economic and energy benefits will be enriched and maintained for future generations of Americans." NHPA was written to create a preservation partnership, among federal agencies and between the national government and state and local governments.

Among the most important elements of NHPA are:

- The creation of the Advisory Council on Historic Preservation

- The establishment of the National Register of Historic Places

- The creation of the network of State Historic Preservation Offices and a commitment to provide federal funds for the operation of those offices

- A process to evaluate whether the expenditure of federal funds has an adverse impact on historic resources. It is called the 106 Review process in reference to the section of the law that created it and is further discussed below.

In 2006, in celebration of the 40th anniversary of NHPA, the Advisory Council on Historic Preservation held a Preservation Summit to recommend changes and improvements in federal government policy toward historic preservation for the next 40 years.

The National Park Service

At the federal level, while there are historic preservation responsibilities across departments, the agency with primary responsibility for America's heritage resources is the National Park Service. The Park Service is a division within the Department of the Interior. In addition to operating the 400 or so national parks, the Park Service is also charged with identifying and maintaining the 27,000 significant structures, 66,000 archeological sites and more than 100 million objects within those parks.

But the responsibilities don't stop with the parks. Within the Park Service is a Cultural Resources division. It is here that most federal historic preservation programs are housed. Among the major federal programs overseen by this agency are the National Register of Historic Places and the Federal Rehabilitation Tax Credit, both of which are discussed below, and HABS/HAER mentioned earlier.

The Park Service also operates the *National Center for Preservation Technology and Training.* NCPTT conducts research directly at its own facilities and provides training on advanced preservation tools and technologies. Through the NCPTT grants program, the Center also funds research and educational efforts by universities, organizations and individuals.

Over the last 25 years the Park Service has also had a *National Heritage Area* (NHA) program. Today there are some 40 NHAs designated by Congress. These are not national parks, but rather collaborations among residents, businesses, governments and non-profit organizations to promote conservation, community revitalization and economic development. The role of the National Park Service is providing technical assistance, planning and limited financial resources. The programs are managed by a non-profit organization or a quasi-public commission. These NHAs, often known as heritage corridors, have proven effective in working across governmental boundaries and in creating regional strategies to more effectively utilize an area's natural and historic resources.

The National Register of Historic Places

The National Register of Historic Places is America's official list of cultural resources worthy of preservation. It is not just individual buildings that are eligible for listing in the National Register but also districts, sites, structures and objects that are determined to be significant.

A resource could be considered significant for different reasons, but generally falls within one or more of four categories:

- Association with events that have made a significant contribution to the broad patterns of American history

- Association with the lives of persons significant in American history

- Distinction based on:
    - type, period or method of construction
    - work of a master
    - high artistic values
    - a significant and distinguishable entity whose components may lack individual distinction

- Have yielded or may be likely to yield information important in prehistory or history.

Although there are some 80,000 listings in the National Register, since many of those listings are districts of buildings and collections of objects, there are more than 1.4 million individual resources recognized including more than one million buildings.

In some countries there is a ranking to given historic resources. In Scotland, for example, there are Category A, B and C buildings. Preservationists in the US have resisted this approach. But there are some sub-sets within the National Register. A property could be identified as a National Historic Landmark, a contributing building in a National Historic Landmark District, an individually listed building in the National Register, or a contributing building in a National Register District. Contributing buildings may not be worthy by themselves of listing, but are recognized as important components of the overall district.

As a general rule, when a building reaches the age of 50, it is appropriate to ask, "Should this be designated as a historic building?" based on one of the above criteria. Being 50 years old doesn't make it historic, but does establish a general time frame for consideration. In cases of exceptional buildings or circumstances, a building might be listed in the National Register even though it is less than 50 years old, but that is rare.

A very important feature of the American system – and decidedly different than most European systems – is that listing in the National Register provides virtually no limitation on what a private owner can do with that property. Listing in the National Register does not keep the owner from altering, adding to or even demolishing the structure. Nearly all protections for historic buildings come at the local level of the government, not the national level. There is one exception. When federal government funds are spent, there needs to be an analysis of whether that expenditure might adversely affect historic resources. This provision is described below under the heading *Section 106*. But other than that, National Register Listing places no restrictions on privately owned historic properties.

What National Register listing does do, however, is provide the avenue through which various incentives may be available. These incentives are also discussed below.

The Secretary's Standards

Formally named *The Secretary of the Interior's Standards and Guidelines for Archeology and Historic Preservation,* but commonly known simply as the *Secretary's Standards,* this document is widely used to determine the appropriate treatment of historic properties. The most frequently cited portion of the *Secretary's Standards* is the Standards for Rehabilitation. (See Appendix B) These are ten commonsense principles to be followed when rehabilitating a historic building. The *Standards* emphasize repair over replacement and the preservation of the qualities for which a property was given historic status. As they are standards for rehabilitation, however, they do accommodate reasonable changes to the property to allow for adaptive reuse. The *Standards* apply to buildings of all periods, styles, materials and sizes and to both the interior and exterior of the building. They also apply to the building's site and environment as well as new additions and related new construction on the site.

There are three instances where the *Secretary's Standards* are most commonly used:

1. They provide guidance to federal agencies on how to treat historic buildings owned by the government;

2. They serve as the design requirements for a property to receive tax credits against federal income tax, which is discussed below; and

3. The *Secretary's Standards* very often serve as the design guidelines for local historic districts which are regulated by local preservation commissions.

But beyond their role in regulatory processes, the *Secretary's Standards* give the basic guidance to architects, builders, developers and property owners on how to best treat historic properties. To supplement the *Standards* the National Park Service has also issued nearly 50 *Preservation Briefs*. These publications cover such diverse topics as *Conserving Energy in Historic Buildings*, *Preservation of Historic Concrete*, *The Maintenance and Repair of Architectural Cast Iron* and *The Preservation and Reuse of Historic Gas Stations*.

The Advisory Council on Historic Preservation

Within the federal government is an independent agency, the Advisory Council on Historic Preservation. Of this 20-member body, half are directly appointed by the President and the rest are members based on the position they hold, such as the Chairman of the National Trust and the Administrator of the Environmental Protection Agency. The members of the Advisory Council are unpaid and meet periodically throughout the year. The day-to-day operations of the Advisory Council are handled by a full-time staff of about 50.

The Advisory Council has several specific roles which include:

- Advising the President and Congress on historic preservation issues

- Recommending legislative and administrative changes at the federal

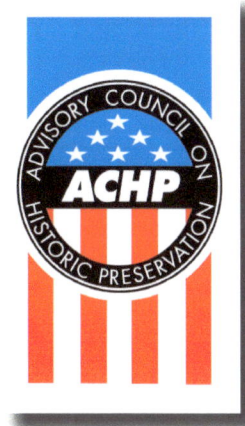

level

- Mediating between local preservation advocates and federal agencies when an action of that agency might adversely affect historic resources (See discussion of Section 106 below)

- Encouraging federal departments to make sure their policies advance historic preservation as required by law

- Acting as advocates and educators on the national level for good historic preservation practices

The General Services Administration (GSA)

The General Services Administration is the landlord for the national government. It is responsible for providing workspace for more than one million federal workers. Of the approximately 340 million square feet of space under GSA's control, about half is in 1,600 government-owned buildings and the balance in 7,500 buildings leased from the private sector.

Of the buildings actually owned by the GSA, roughly half are over 50 years old and half of those (or just over 400) are identified as "historic."

To ensure that the historic buildings are treated appropriately, the GSA has a special Historic Buildings Center. This office is responsible for assuring compliance with federal law regarding heritage structures. But the Historic Buildings Center also comes up with solutions for preservation challenges such as retrofitting historic buildings to meet security needs without compromising the architectural integrity, and adding fire suppression systems and handicapped access while still meeting good preservation design standards.

> Two excellent publications by the GSA which explain their approach to historic resources are available online.
>
> *Held in Public Trust: PBS Strategy for Using Historic Buildings*
>
> http://www.gsa.gov/gsa/cm_attachments/GSA_DOCUMENT/HIPT_R2-u3Z_0Z5RDZ-i34K-pR.pdf
>
> and
>
> *Extending the Legacy: GSA Historic Building Stewardship*
>
> http://www.gsa.gov/gsa/cm_attachments/GSA_DOCUMENT/Stewardship_R2-vMR_0Z5RDZ-i34K-pR.pdf

In recent years the GSA has become an active participant in public-private partnerships concerned with heritage buildings, which are described later in this report.

The National Environmental Policy Act (NEPA)

In 1970, Congress passed and the President signed the National Environmental Policy Act. While the major focus of the act relates to the natural environment, there is a provision that plays an important role in protecting the historic built environment. NEPA requires that whenever a significant federal action is undertaken, an *Environmental Impact Study* (EIS) must be conducted. While the EIS looks at such things as impact on water quality and endangered species, it also must consider any potential impact on historic resources. If an adverse impact is identified, then the federal agency must either alter its plans or provide ways to mitigate the negative effects.

Section 106

Section 106 refers to that portion of the National Historic Preservation Act. This provision requires that any time federal government funds are spent – by a federal government agency directly, or by a recipient of federal funds (a state or local government, for example) there has to be a determination on whether that expenditure would have an adverse effect on historic resources. So, for example, if a state department of transportation was widening a road and part of the funds to do so came from the federal government, the transportation department would have to consider the effect the new highway would have on nearby archeological resources.

Section 106 requires a five-step process:

1. Identify and evaluate any historic properties that may be affected

2. Assess the effects (no effect, no adverse effect, or adverse effect)

3. Consultation

4. Comment by the Advisory Council on Historic Preservation

5. Proceed

At each stage of the process there are opportunities for input from the State Historic Preservation Officer and the public.

While Section 106 does not in the end require that all historic resources be saved, the goal is to reach a Memorandum of Agreement in the consultation stages wherein interested parties will agree to a plan to avoid, reduce or mitigate any adverse effect.

While most often a Section 106 process arises when federal money is being spent, it could also occur as a result of other activities such as the federal government leasing a property, rehabilitating a building or issuing a license.

The US State Department and the Ambassador's Fund

The US State Department is charged with managing America's relationships with foreign governments, international organizations and the people of other countries. This diplomacy takes many forms. One of those forms is a small but important program – the Ambassador's Fund for Cultural Preservation. This is the only program in the US government that provides direct small-grant support to heritage preservation in less-developed countries. Nearly 120 countries have been identified as being eligible for Ambassador's Fund awards. These projects generally come either through cooperation with the host country's Ministry of Culture or through a preservation-oriented NGO.

Conservation of the 10th century Temple of Phnom Bahkeng, Cambodia. Cultural Heritage Center.
Received $978,705 grant in 2008.

Historic Preservation and the Courts

In the American system, there are three co-equal branches of government: the Executive (the President and the federal departments), the Legislative (Congress) and the Judicial (the court system). As a general rule the legislative branch passes laws and it is up to the executive branch to enforce them. Courts ordinarily would not be involved unless there is a question as to whether a particular law is consistent with the Constitution.

Fortunately there has been a major decision by the United States Supreme Court supporting historic preservation laws. In *Penn Central Transportation Company versus New York City*, the court held that the regulation of privately owned property that had been designated as historic was a legitimate and constitutionally allowable activity of government.

The States and Historic Preservation

Throughout American history the states have been seen as the basic element of all three levels of government. Indeed it is no accident that the nation itself is called the United States – signifying a nation composed of a federation of smaller units of government. Each state has its own constitution, and some of them specifically identify historic preservation as a public-sector responsibility. For example, the Virginia constitution states that, "it shall be the policy of the Commonwealth to conserve, develop, and utilize its natural resources, its public lands, and its historical sites and buildings."

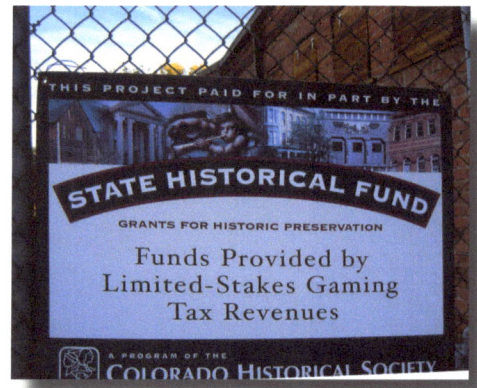

**State Historical Fund
Colorado**

State Historic Preservation Offices

While each state has the right to establish its own historic preservation policies, the passage of the National Historic Preservation Act created the framework within which each state operates today. Although the NHPA was federal-level legislation, it created a network of state-level units called State Historic Preservation Offices (SHPO). Though the SHPOs were created by national legislation, they are very much part of state government and answerable to the legislatures and the governors of each individual state. But the National Historic Preservation Act was, from the beginning, intended to be create a partnership among national, state and local governments. The SHPO is the state-level partner.

Each of the states has a SHPO, as do the District of Columbia and eight territories of the United States. The SHPO has been delegated authority from the national level, but also may have specific additional responsibilities assigned at the state level. The primary roles as spelled out in the NHPA are:

- Survey historic properties and maintain an inventory of heritage resources

- Nominate properties to the National Register and administer National Register nominations that are submitted by others

- Prepare statewide preservation plans

- Administer grant programs, including those funded by the federal government

- Review and comment on all projects submitted for Federal Rehabilitation Tax Credits

- Review and comment on all projects that are subject to Section 106 provisions regarding any impact of the projects on historic resources

- Provide technical assistance, information, education and training on historic preservation to the public and private sectors on historic preservation responsibilities and opportunities.

- Encourage the creation of local historic districts and assist local governments to become Certified Local Governments (CLGs) (described below).

In recognition of their being delegated responsibilities from the federal government, each of the SHPOs receives an annual appropriation to compensate them for that work. Typically around half of the SHPO's budget comes from federal dollars, the balance from an appropriation by the state legislature.

Native American tribes have autonomous jurisdiction over numerous functions within Tribal boundaries. Among those is the right to assume the responsibilities of the SHPO on Tribal lands. Currently, nearly 80 tribes have chosen to do so. These are called Tribal Historic Preservation Offices (THPO).

Other State Legislation

Beyond the existence of a State Historic Preservation Office, however, the different states have a great variety of policies toward historic preservation. Around 40 states have State Registers of Historic Places with their own set of criteria for listing. A majority of the states have some regulations related to the consideration of the impact of state expenditures on historic resources; however, few are as effective at the state level as the Section 106 process on the national level.

California has an environmental law known as CEQA, the California Environmental Quality Act. This legislation requires an Environmental Impact Study (EIS) for major projects of both the public and private sectors. But "environment" under the act is defined as "the physical conditions which exist within the area which will be affected by a proposed project, including land, air, water, minerals, flora, fauna, noise, objects of historic or aesthetic significance." The State of Connecticut has similar provisions in its Environmental Policy Act.

But the states are not limited in their approach to historic preservation to using the "stick" of regulation. More than 30 states also use the "carrot" of some form of incentives to encourage the investment of private capital into historic buildings. Examples of those incentives are described below.

So while the principle of federalism allows states great leeway in policy matters, all states have Historic Preservation Offices and more and more are recognizing the importance of heritage resources to the economic, social and cultural wealth of their state.

Local Government

The discussion of the roles of national and state governments has been lengthy because of the multiple programs and the relative complexity of preservation policy at those levels. But in the United States, it is really at the local government level where meaningful protections of historic properties exist.

In the United States, the authority for local governments to act is created by state legislatures in what is commonly called enabling legislation. Every state has passed enabling legislation to allow local governments to establish what are generally called historic district commissions, preservation commissions or landmarks commissions. The state law also spells out the powers that such commissions might have.

Preservation Commissions

It is then the right (but not the obligation) of local governments to create historic district commissions. Today there are approximately 3,500 local preservation commissions in the United States. The specific powers of these commissions vary widely, both because of the authority granted in each state's enabling legislation, but also based on the attitudes and perspectives of the local city council that creates the commissions. Some, such as New York City's Landmarks Commission, have significant powers over identified historic resources there. At the other end of the spectrum are some small communities where the role of the preservation commission is advisory only.

Powers of Commissions

But a typical example might be the powers for the Historical Landmarks Commission for the city of Portland, Oregon. They are as follows:

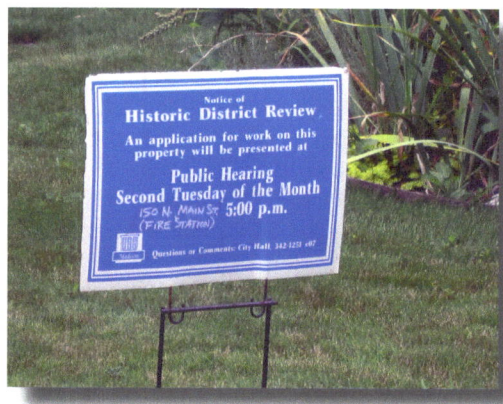

Madison, Georgia

- Recommend to the City Council the designation of individual buildings as landmarks

- Recommend to the City Council the establishment of historic districts

- Develop and recommend to the City Council design guidelines for properties within historic districts

- Review and provide comment on development proposals within historic districts

- Review proposals for demolition requests in historic districts

- Provide advice to city government, City Council and the general public on preservation issues

- Conduct educational outreach

Most local ordinances specify that for actions such as creating historic districts or designating individual landmarks, the preservation commission makes a recommendation but the City Council must rule on that recommendation. For actions such as approving changes, additions or alterations to properties within historic districts, generally the commission itself makes the decision.

Property Owner Appeals

There must be some avenue of appeal if a property owner is dissatisfied with the decision of a preservation commission. Appeals typically may be made either to the local planning commission or the City Council. Under American law there is nearly always an opportunity to appeal commission decisions to the court system. But unless the property owner could demonstrate that the commission itself violated its own procedures and statutory authority, or that it acted in an arbitrary manner, courts would generally uphold the decision of the preservation commission and the City Council.

Makeup of the Commission

The membership of the commission is also determined by local ordinances. Again, Portland provides a typical example.

- Eight members, seven appointed by the Mayor and confirmed by the City Council and one by the chair of the planning commission

- Four year terms, with a maximum of two terms

- One member must also be a member of the planning commission

- One local historian, one architect, one architectural historian

- Two members with expertise in any of the following: landscape architecture, real estate, construction, community development, urban planning, archeology, law, finance, cultural geography, cultural anthropology

- Two members at large

Districts versus Individual Landmarks

Nearly every local preservation ordinance gives the power to the commission to designate individual properties as local landmarks. And in cities such as New York, that authority is commonly used. However, in the United States probably 90% of all the properties that receive some sort of protection under local preservation laws are protected because of their location within a local historic district rather than because they have been designated as individual landmarks.

Commission Effectiveness

The effectiveness of local preservation commissions in protecting heritage resources varies, of course. It will vary based on the state enabling legislation, on the specifics of the local ordinance, on the political commitment to preservation of the City Council, on the strength of local heritage advocates, and other factors. But when local commissions are most effective there seem to be common denominators: 1) there are clear, written, illustrated guidelines for property owners to follow; 2) the commission is firm but consistent in its decisions; 3) there is staff available with whom a property owner can discuss issues prior to having to formally appear before the commission; and 4) there is ongoing educational outreach by the commission and its staff to property owners, the real estate and banking communities, construction companies and community activists.

Design Guidelines

All good preservation commissions have established design guidelines. While most use the *Secretary's Standards for Rehabilitation* as the local guidelines, some cities have written their own set of guidelines to reflect the special conditions and peculiarities of their historic districts. It should also be noted that very few local preservation commissions are involved in regulating the interior of a building; their primary concern is for those portions of the building that have a public exposure.

In most cases the preservation commission would have review over both the rehabilitation of the historic buildings in the district and also any new construction. Often design guidelines have special sections for new infill construction within the district boundaries. When a project is approved it is awarded what is typically called a Certificate of Appropriateness.

Certified Local Governments

It was mentioned earlier that the National Historic Preservation Act was written to create a partnership among levels of government. Local governments, too, have a place in that partnership through a program called Certified Local Governments (CLGs). Of the 3,500 local preservation commissions, nearly half – around 1,600 – are also designated as Certified Local Governments. This designation is awarded by the State Historic Preservation Office. The minimum requirements are: 1) having a local preservation ordinance; 2) having a preservation commission; 3) maintaining an active survey of local historic resources; and 4) participating in the National Register process by submitting or reviewing nominations. Some states will establish additional standards for the CLG designation.

Once designated, CLGs are eligible to receive limited funding. Each SHPO is required to pass through at least 10% of the funds it receives from the National Park Service to the CLGs. Those local commissions can use those moneys for surveys, preparation of design guidelines, training for commissioners and staff, or in the rehabilitation of National Register properties.

Preservation Is Local

There is an old saying in the United States that all politics are local. To a large extent in America nearly all preservation is local as well. There are both advantages and disadvantages of this approach compared to the national, centralized systems of other countries. But this bottom-up approach is consistent with American history and the principle of federalism, and keeps decisions regarding historic properties in the hands of local citizens who know these places best.

The Private Sector

For historic preservation in the United States, the public sector sets the rules, keeps the inventories and provides incentives. But active preservation is an overwhelmingly private sector activity.

In broad categories the private sector's role in historic preservation is on three levels: 1) ownership of historic buildings; 2) investment in historic structures; and 3) donations to support non-profit preservation activities.

Private Sector Ownership

In the category of ownership, over half of National Historic Landmarks are owned by the private sector. Probably in excess of 80% of all buildings on the National Register and 90% of buildings in local historic districts are in private hands. There simply are neither the financial resources nor the political support for any level of government to be the primary owner of historic properties. While governments are expected to be good stewards of the historic buildings they do own, it is broadly seen that it is the private sector to which the ownership, maintenance and management of historic buildings belongs.

Private Sector Investment

Because "historic preservation" is not a discrete category in any economic statistics, it is impossible to give an exact amount that is spent each year on the rehabilitation and maintenance of historic buildings. Here is what is known: In recent years the amount invested in the rehabilitation of historic buildings that took advantage of the Federal Rehabilitation Tax Credit ranged between $3 billion and $4.5 billion annually. The Rehabilitation Tax Credit program is discussed below. Conservatively, the total investment in historic rehabilitation is 3.5 to 4 times the amount spent in these tax credit projects. This means that there is probably between $10 and $20 billion spent each year on rehabilitating historic buildings in the United States, the vast majority of that by the private sector.

Private Sector Donations

But it is also the private sector that, through donations, supports the work of non-profit preservation organizations. The National Trust for Historic Preservation – the largest of the non-profit preservation organizations – in recent years has received between $20 million and $35 million each year in contributions from individuals and corporations. Millions more has been given to state and local preservation organizations, historic house museums, and other preservation causes. The historic preservation version of Tocqueville's "voluntary associations" are largely financed by contributions from the private sector without which they simply could not exist.

Non-Profit Organizations and Historic Preservation

What most of the world calls NGOs, non-governmental organizations, in the United States are usually known as non-profit organizations. These non-profits are also occasionally referred to as the *third sector*, the other two being the public and private sectors.

As was pointed out earlier, throughout the history of the United States, these organizations have played a major role in virtually every part of American life. They are particularly important in the historic preservation movement.

At the national, state and local levels there are literally thousands of non-profit organizations with historic preservation as a major focus of their activities. While these activities vary widely, they generally fall into five categories: education, advocacy, ownership and management of historic buildings, participation in the development of heritage properties and various programs. Programs include such activities as giving awards, hosting annual preservation celebrations, identifying historic properties, tours of historic places and many others.

Non-Profit Preservation Organizations at the National Level

The National Trust for Historic Preservation

The premier non-profit organization in the United States is the National Trust for Historic Preservation. The National Trust operates from a headquarters in Washington, DC, and a network of nine regional offices. The National Trust has an annual budget of around $70 million, 320 full-time employees and 270,000 members. The Trust also has built up an endowment (almost exclusively from the donations from corporations and individuals) of more than $200 million, the earnings on which provide 10 to 15% of the annual operating budget. As the largest preservation organization, the National Trust is involved in all

The National Trust Washington, DC

the areas noted above.

Education

In the area of education the Trust conducts training courses and workshops for heritage professionals and holds an annual conference which some 2500 preservationists – professionals and laypersons alike – attend. The Trust has published more than a hundred books and monographs on a wide range of preservation issues, including: *Preservation of Historic Burial Grounds, Layperson's Guide to Preservation Law, Effective Communications for Preservation Nonprofits,* and *Better Models for Urban Supermarkets.* The Trust also publishes the quarterly *Forum Journal* for heritage professionals and other leaders and the widely acclaimed *Preservation* magazine, a bimonthly publication for members.

Advocacy

On the advocacy side, the National Trust has departments of public policy and law which both advance policy positions and are sometimes directly involved in litigation on issues that could have an impact on preservation nationwide. Policy initiatives in recent years have included the anti-sprawl program *Smart Growth,* of which the Trust was an early participant in a national effort, initiatives to promote adaptive reuse of historic buildings for affordable housing and, most recently, efforts to document and publicize the role of historic preservation to environmental sustainability

Also considered advocacy would be the Trust's annual list of America's 11 Most Endangered Historic Places. Widely publicized in the mainstream media, eleven heritage assets from around the country are identified as being at significant risk of loss. Some of the Most Endangered Places are significant individual properties imminently in danger from demolition by bulldozer or by neglect. Others are categories of properties, a recent example being historic places in seven eastern states being adversely affected by transmission line corridors. Finally, some properties are often chosen as much for their reflection of a larger issue as for the nature of the particular property. For example Brooklyn, New York's industrial waterfront was a recent listing, but reflected the loss of that particular type of heritage asset in dozens of places in the US.

Programs

It is probably on the program side that the National Trust is best known. Programs are multiple and diverse including:

- *Preservation Services Fund* grants to help pay for feasibility studies, guest speakers or promotional materials by local preservation groups, preservation planning, or intervention for a preservation emergency.

- *Dozen Distinctive Destinations*, an annual list of communities that have retained their character and unique historic quality.

- *Rural Heritage Development Initiative* promoting the use of historic resources in two predominantly rural states.

- *Save America's Treasures*, a federal public-private partnership program for which the Trust was the administrator

- *National Main Street Center*, the most widely known program of the National Trust which is further discussed below.

Properties

On the property side, the National Trust has a collection of 29 properties in 13 states and the District of Columbia. These range from the homes of Presidents Madison and Wilson to the 1806 African Meeting House in Boston to one of the finest examples of modern residential architecture, the Glass House in Connecticut. Although the US National Trust was based on the National Trust of England, Scotland and Wales and originally conceived as primarily a property holding organization, its role in 60 years has significantly evolved. Property ownership and management is still certainly important, but is no longer the primary focus that it was in the National Trust's earliest days.

**Woodlawn
Alexandria, Virginia**

Real Estate Development

Direct participation in the development and reuse of historic properties is a role some preservation organizations at all levels have undertaken. The National Trust does this through a for-profit subsidiary called the National Trust Community Investment Corporation. Though wholly owned by the Trust, this independent corporation invests in historic property developments, usually in partnership with banks, investors, property owners and developers. Like any for-profit entity, it pays taxes on any profit it may make. But the earnings after taxes are paid then flow back to the National Trust to support its ongoing operations.

Other National Non-Profit Preservation Organizations

There are other national preservation organizations as well. *Preservation Action*, discussed earlier, is a grassroots lobbying and advocacy organization based in Washington, DC. *US/ICOMOS* is the national chapter of the International Council on Monuments and Sites, the international NGO made up of professionals in the heritage field. US/ICOMOS is one of the largest national committees. The *National Alliance of Preservation Commissions* is a group whose members are local historic district commissions. NAPC conducts annual training programs for preservation commissioners and keeps a database of various local preservation ordinances and design guidelines. The SHPOs have their own national organization called the *National Conference of State Historic Preservation Officers* (NCSHPO) which represents their interests in Washington, DC. *The National Preservation Institute* provides workshops, seminars and customized training sessions on a wide range of cultural management and regulatory issues.

While these are separate, independent organizations, they try to work together to advance broader policy aims. Together they form the national network of NGO preservation institutions.

Non-Profit Preservation Organizations at the State Level

Just as the public sector side of historic preservation in America is divided on the national, state and local basis, so is the NGO sector. At the state level, some 40 of the 50 states have statewide preservation education and advocacy organizations. The vast majority of these organizations have a full-time staff. The size and functions of these organizations, however, range widely— from a one-person operation with a very limited budget to large entities with considerable human and financial resources and significant political and social influence.

Indiana Landmarks

In the latter category is Indiana Landmarks. Founded in 1960, the organization is now the largest statewide preservation organization in the country with a staff of 50 located in its headquarters in the state capital of Indianapolis and nine regional offices throughout the state. Indiana Landmarks is involved in all five of the non-profit roles including education, advocacy, programs, ownership and management of properties, and direct real estate investment. The grant and loan programs of Indiana Landmarks have ultimately been responsible for the preservation of hundreds of Indiana historic properties.

Preservation North Carolina

Another national model of a statewide preservation organization is Preservation North Carolina (PNC). This 60-year-old organization operates on an annual budget of around $2 million. Of this amount around half comes from donations from corporations and the organization's 4,000 members.

PNC's best-known program is the Endangered Properties Fund. Sometimes called a "revolving fund," this program acquires historic properties – often through gift or nominal purchase price from the current owners – and resells them with protective covenants (see sidebar). Over the years this program has saved more than 500 historic North Carolina properties and has generated private investment of an estimated $200 million.

Non-Profit Preservation Organizations at the Local Level

There are literally thousands of local preservation organizations in communities in every part of the United States. Most are all-volunteer organizations with no staff and limited budgets. Some own and operate a local house museum or local historic site. Others are Main Street boards using historic preservation as the vehicle for economic development in downtowns and neighborhood commercial centers. All are citizen-based organizations committed to identifying and preserving the local community's historic resources.

Preservation Resource Center of New Orleans

One such organization is the Preservation Resource Center of New Orleans (PRC). In 1974 a group of New Orleans citizens became concerned that in spite of the city having long-standing preservation commission and some of the most important historic buildings and neighborhoods in America, too much was being lost to the bulldozer, to abandonment and to demolition by neglect. Thus with an annual budget of $100,000 and two staff persons, PRC was created.

Protecting Historic Properties

In the United States, protection for historic properties can come about in two ways. The first is protection through a local preservation ordinance, as was discussed earlier. The second method is through restrictions placed on the title to the property itself. These might be through what are known as deed restrictions or through preservation easements. These restrictions limit what can be done to the property, require approvals from a public or non-profit organization whenever changes are being proposed, and are binding not only on the current owner but on all subsequent owners.

So that properties are protected into the future, Preservation North Carolina places this type of restriction on the title to the property before the organization sells it to a new owner.

Preservation North Carolina has also been directly involved in complex historic redevelopment projects. Notable in this regard is the Edenton Cotton Mill Village. This former textile complex was mostly vacant and deteriorating when PNC acquired it through a donation from the mill's owners in 1996. The property has been fully redeveloped and now is a national award winning model as a sustainable cottage community.

Today PRC employs 45 full- and part-time staff and has an annual total budget of $6 million. PRC is, in partnership with others, leading the recovery from Hurricane Katrina by assuring that historic resources are at the center of recovery efforts. One such effort is *Operation Comeback,* which works to get historic houses in the hands of first-time homeowners. It does this through a combination of training and financial assistance. In some instances PRC directly acquires dilapidated properties, rehabilitates them and then sells them to a committed owner. Special financing programs are directed to New Orleans' police and firefighters.

Another program is a direct response to those displaced by Hurricane Katrina – *Rebuilding Together New Orleans*. Through a partnership program with a national non-profit organization, PRC is working to bring back to New Orleans citizens who had owned historic houses that had been severely damaged by the hurricane. More than 100 houses have so far been rehabilitated and dozens more rehabs are in progress.

New Orleans is a city with great African-American, Cajun and Creole cultural traditions, especially in food, music and architecture. PRC's *Ethnic Heritage Preservation Program* is documenting and creating a database of the important sites of New Orleans jazz history, installing plaques on homes of the greats of jazz, and has so far restored two houses of these jazz pioneers. Most of these structures wouldn't meet the test of being architectural masterpieces. But they are important physical representations of the culture in one of America's oldest cities.

The Network of Historic Preservation NGOs

The network of historic preservation non-profit organizations exists at the national, state and local levels. Through this network of "voluntary associations" millions of individual citizens have made historic preservation a part of their daily lives.

How Historic Preservation Strengthens Communities in the United States

As in most countries, the historic preservation movement in the United States began with efforts to save the estates of important historical figures and the mansions of the rich. The movement was accelerated when more buildings of significant architectural and aesthetic quality were being lost. And important historic and architectural monuments are still a key type of resource that preservationists try to save.

But in the last three decades, historic preservation has moved from being an end in itself – save old buildings in order to save old buildings – to a broad-based effort to protect heritage assets as means toward wider and more diverse ends. The story of this evolution is best told by examples from around America.

Historic Preservation and Affordable Housing

Historic preservation in the United States is not just for the rich. Historic preservation is part of the daily lives of Americans at all economic levels—and, notably, for those in need of affordable housing.

In recent years a third of all the housing units created or rehabilitated using the Federal Rehabilitation Tax Credit have been for low- and moderate-income residents. The Historic Tax Credit is often paired with a separate provision in federal tax law that provides credits in exchange for investing in affordable housing. These projects are not just creating units that are affordable; they are creating quality units in historic structures that have meaning to the local community.

In Arkansas, *The Arc* is a non-profit organization whose mission is to provide support, advocacy, education and affordable housing to those with disabilities. It is also The Arc's goal to integrate this housing and its residents into the mainstream community. In the last few years The Arc has invested over $30 million in development including the rehabilitation of eight historic buildings. Historic preservation is not the mission of The Arc, but it has proven an excellent way of fulfilling its mission.

HUD is the acronym for the Department of Housing and Urban Development of the US Government. HUD's mission is "to increase homeownership, support community development and increase access to affordable housing free from discrimination." To meet that mission, HUD has numerous programs for local governments and housing providers including grants, loans, loan guarantees and other assistance.

But HUD has also learned that sometimes it can best fulfill its goals through the use of historic buildings. In fact there is an annual HUD Secretary's Award for Excellence in Historic Preservation. A recent winner of that prestigious award was the Midtown Exchange in downtown Minneapolis, Minnesota. This 1928 former department store and office complex had sat vacant and deteriorating for a number of years. Today it is a vibrant mixed-use center in Minneapolis and includes seven floors of rental apartments, eight floors of condominiums and nine floors of office space.

A project of this size is obviously complex with multiple ownership and financing participants. Out of the $192 million in costs, in excess of $16 million came from various HUD programs. The State of Minnesota and several units of local government also provided funding support. The project utilized Federal Rehabilitation Tax Credits, low-income housing tax credits and other federal tax incentives.

This one project had three goals: historic preservation, development of affordable housing, and inner-city redevelopment. After having been an eyesore for a decade, the Midtown Exchange has now become a new multifunctional heart of downtown Minneapolis.

Not every project is the size of the Midtown Exchange, however. The City of West Hollywood, California has identified providing affordable housing as one of its primary goals. How to reach that goal? One answer has been to convert the small, obsolete Fire Station #7 into three apartment units for low-income families. This project was a complex public-private partnership wherein the County of Los Angeles donated the property to the City of West Hollywood, on the condition that the structure be used for affordable housing. The City then conveyed the building to the Los Angeles Housing Partnership to undertake the development and management. Today three West Hollywood families have housing they can afford in the rehabilitated historic Fire Station #7.

With scarce resources, innovative government officials look for ways to fulfill multiple responsibilities with a single expenditure. In both of the examples above, governments at every level made the decision not just to provide affordable housing, or just to help urban revitalization, or just to save heritage assets. Those governments and their private and non-profit sector partners made the decision to do all of those things – through the adaptive reuse of historic buildings.

The Betty Ruth and Milton B. Hollander Foundation Center, at 410 Asylum Street, Hartford
Affordable housing units added: 56

Historic Preservation for Downtown Renewal

For nearly 40 years after World War II, downtowns in towns and cities across America were in decline. Suburbanization of housing, corporate office parks at the edges of cities, state and national highway systems, housing policy, regional shopping centers and increased automobile ownership all contributed to downtown's decline. Left behind were vacant and underutilized historic buildings.

But over the last 20 years, downtowns of every size in every part of the country have experienced a remarkable recovery. While the strategies, the pace of change and the magnitude of the investment will differ, there is one common denominator – virtually every sustained success story in downtown revitalization has had historic preservation as a key component of the effort. The relative importance of preservation as part of downtown revitalization will vary some, depending on the local resources, the age of the city, the strength of the local preservation advocacy groups and the enlightenment of the leadership. But downtown revitalization with no historic preservation? It simply isn't happening.

Larimer Square, Denver, Colorado

An excellent example is St. Louis, Missouri. Downtown St. Louis had experienced decades of decline and population loss. But over the last ten years, led by efforts of the Downtown St. Louis Partnership, there has been a dramatic change. More than $4 billion has been invested, 90 new retail businesses have opened, 2,500 new hotel rooms have been created and 5,000 new residents now call downtown St. Louis home.

There has certainly been sizeable investment in new construction, including a $387 million stadium and a $220 million federal courthouse. But the vast majority of the projects and nearly half of the total investment dollars have gone into the rehabilitation of historic buildings. In fact, nearly 100 vacant or abandoned historic buildings have been rehabilitated into hotels, offices, apartment buildings, retail facilities and condominiums. Just the 15 largest historic preservation projects represent private investment of more than $1 billion.

St. Louis may be the biggest turnaround story of American downtowns. And it has accomplished this transformation by utilizing its historic asserts.

Historic Preservation for Small Town Revitalization

The Economic Development Administration (EDA) is a federal agency whose mission is "to lead the federal economic development agenda by promoting innovation and competitiveness, preparing American regions for growth and success in the worldwide economy." Among EDA's activities is a series of annual awards for excellence in economic development efforts. The awards are in such categories as Enhancing Regional Competitiveness, Rural Economic Development, Technology-led Economic Development, and Innovation in Economic Development.

In 2008 EDA added a category called Excellence in Historic Preservation-led Strategies to Enhance Economic Development, in recognition of the successful role historic preservation can play in economic development. The first award winner was the Main Street program of Silver City, New Mexico, population 10,000. Using its historic resources as the base, Silver City has gone from having well over half of its downtown buildings empty to having a 90% occupancy rate and more than 170 businesses of all types, and has created an economic climate favorable for both new businesses to open and existing businesses to expand.

Historic Preservation for Economic Development

For proponents of local economic development there are many measures of success, but near the top of the list are: 1) numbers of jobs created and 2) increased household income that those jobs generate. When these are considered in combination, very few economic activities of any kind have more local impact than does the rehabilitation of historic buildings.

Madison, Georgia

In the United States, as a general rule, half of the budget for new construction will be spent on labor and the other half on materials. The budget for rehabilitation, on the other hand, will be 60 to 70 % spent on labor with the balance being on materials. This labor intensity affects a local economy on two levels. First, the materials are likely to be purchased from across the country or around the world, but the services of the plumber, the electrician and the carpenter are purchased from across the street. Further, once the carpet is installed, the carpet does not spend any more money. But the plumber gets a haircut on the way home, buys groceries and joins the local health club – each recirculating that paycheck within the community.

Economic development is often considered in terms of manufacturing, so that is a good comparison. In a typical US state like Iowa, for example, for every million dollars of production, the average manufacturing firm creates 10.7 jobs. A million dollars in new construction creates 19.8 jobs. But that same million dollars in the rehabilitation of a historic building? 21.1 jobs.

In Iowa a million dollars of manufacturing in output will add, on average, about $406,000 to local household incomes. A million dollars of new construction will add $622,000. But a million dollars of rehabilitation? Over $682,000. Now of course the argument can be made, "But once you've built the building the job creation is done." Yes, but there are two responses to that. First, real estate is a capital asset – like a drill press or a boxcar. It has an economic impact during construction, but a subsequent economic impact when it is in productive use. Additionally, however, since most building components have a life of between 25 and 40 years, a community could rehabilitate 2 to 3 % of its building stock per year and have perpetual employment in the building trades.

Historic Preservation for Small Business Incubation

America is a country of small business. While it is usually the *Fortune 500* that make headlines in the *Wall Street Journal,* 85% of all net new jobs are created by small businesses. One of the few costs firms of that size can control is occupancy costs – rents. In both downtowns and in neighborhood commercial districts, a major contribution to the local economy is the relative affordability of older buildings. It is no accident that the creative, imaginative, small startup firms are not located in the corporate office "campus," the industrial park or the shopping center – they simply cannot afford the rents there. Older and historic commercial buildings provide the needed space, nearly always with no subsidy or assistance of any kind to the occupants.

Pioneer Square in Seattle is one of the great historic commercial neighborhoods in America. The business management association there did a survey to find out why Pioneer Square businesses chose that neighborhood. The most common answer? That it was a historic district. The second most common answer? The cost of occupancy. Neither of those responses is accidental.

Historic Preservation for Tourism

Internationally, heritage-based tourism is among the fastest growing segments of the rapidly growing tourism sector. Two important lessons have been learned in both the United States and elsewhere about the economic impact of heritage visitors as compared to tourists in general:

1. Heritage visitors tend to stay longer, visit more places during their stay and spend more per day. Therefore the per visit economic impact is decidedly greater than for tourists in general.

2. When visiting a historic site, only 8 to 12% of the visitor expenditure is at the site itself, with the balance spent in local restaurants, hotels, retail shops and on transportation. So while the historic site may have been the magnet to attract the visitor, other businesses were the major beneficiaries.

Savannah, Georgia

Many cities in the United States have capitalized on their historic resources to attract heritage visitors. One of the most successful is Savannah, Georgia. Savannah was founded in 1733 and is America's first planned city. It was laid out around 24 original squares, 21 of which are still in existence. In 1966 the 1.1 square mile core of old Savannah was named a National Historic Landmark District – the largest in the country.

In recent years Savannah has reinvested in its historic buildings, neighborhoods, and downtown to capitalize on its historic resources to attract heritage visitors. That investment has certainly paid off. Tourism has been increasing in Savannah about 7% per year with expenditures rising at an even greater rate. 80% percent of the 6½ million annual visitors to Savannah come for leisure purposes, and the historic resources are far and away the biggest attraction.

This increased level of tourism has had a significant impact on two different segments of the local economy. As might be expected, there has been sizable growth in numbers employed in the hospitality industry itself, with direct jobs in that sector exceeding 29,000. But the growth of that industry has catalyzed investment in historic buildings, so employment in the construction trades has grown as well.

Heritage tourism is not the right strategy for every historic town, and can have negative as well as positive effects if not well managed. But Savannah, Georgia has become one of the favorite heritage destinations in America and the local economic benefits are widespread, including generating $290 million each year in federal, state and local tax revenue.

Historic Preservation for the Arts

There is something about historic buildings that make them seem appropriate for the arts. Many of the great art museums in the world are in some of the greatest heritage buildings in the world – the Louvre, the Hermitage, the Prado. The same is true in the United States, with great collections housed in historic buildings such as the Metropolitan Museum in New York, the Art Institute in Chicago and the National Gallery in Washington, DC.

Ann Arbor, Michigan

But on a totally different level, historic buildings are being used by towns and cities to build an arts community locally. Paducah, Kentucky is such a place. Paducah is a town of 27,000 situated on the Ohio River. Its oldest neighborhood – Lowertown – has a great collection of century-old houses. But it also had high vacancy rates, high crime rates, low levels of maintenance and low property values. So an initiative by the City of Paducah and local banks was begun to change that neighborhood, and they decided to do it with the arts.

In 2000, Paducah established the Artist Relocation Program to attract painters, sculptors, weavers, printmakers, photographers from around the country to move to their small city. The City used changes in zoning requirements, a generous financing program, excellent marketing, and those historic houses as the bait. To date some 70 artists from across the US have chosen to make Paducah their new home. They have invested in those historic structures, turning them into live-work space, cafes, galleries and studios. The neighborhood is now alive with creativity, energy and reinvestment. Establishing a "creative class" in Paducah was the goal, but the historic Lowertown neighborhood was the means of reaching the goal.

Main Street – Economic Development in the Context of Historic Preservation

Main Street is a program of the National Trust for Historic Preservation. In the 30 years since this program was developed more than 2,500 communities in all 50 states have had Main Street programs. A Main Street program utilizes the historic buildings in downtowns and neighborhood commercial centers as the vehicle for the economic revitalization of those areas. It does so through a comprehensive approach to revitalization that includes a volunteer organization, promotional activities, design efforts including the rehabilitation of the historic buildings, and economic restructuring of the downtown or neighborhood economy.

Salina, Colorado

The Main Street approach is by far the most cost effective program of economic development of any kind in the United States, typically leveraging more than $27 dollars of investment for each dollar spent by the public sector in support of the program. Over the last 25 years, $45 billion dollars have been spent on physical improvements in Main Street districts, including nearly 200,000 building renovation and construction projects. Over that time 83,000 new businesses have been established in Main Street districts creating more than 370,000 net new jobs.

Preservation Education

**Preservation workshop
Windsor, Vermont**

In the last 30 years in the United States, historic preservation has grown in the amount of activity and in complexity. This has led to the corresponding need for trained professionals and the emergence of formal education in the preservation field. Earlier were noted training programs of the National Trust, the National Preservation Institute and the National Park Service.

But preservation is now a curriculum option within the formal college and university systems. Eight colleges, both public and private, offer undergraduate degrees in historic preservation with others providing options for a minor or a certificate in preservation

On the graduate level there are even more choices, with nearly 25 universities having programs leading to a master's degree in historic preservation. Another 25 have preservation emphases within programs of planning, art history, architecture or related fields.

There is also active formal training in the "hands-on" side of heritage conservation including both two- and four-year programs. At any given time between 1,500 and 1,800 students are enrolled in degree-granting historic preservation programs in the United States.

The National Council for Preservation Education is a network of these programs that serves as a source of information on various options available.

The Importance of Adaptive Reuse

The principle of adaptive reuse is central to historic preservation theory and practice in the United States. There is an old saying in real estate that far more buildings are torn down than fall down. But why would a building be torn down? The four most frequent reasons are these: 1) the site could be developed much more intensively, the value of the land if vacant being greater than the land with the existing building in place; 2) the use for which the building was built no longer exists, or no longer exists in that form; 3) the mechanical systems or the building configuration no longer meet the efficiency or utility needs of the marketplace; or 4) the building has suffered from significant deferred maintenance.

One response to each of those reasons is demolition. The other response, and the environmentally and socially responsible response, is adaptive reuse. It was noted earlier that historic preservation in the United States is overwhelmingly a private sector activity. But for private sector capital to be invested there has to be some form of return from that investment – either in rents received from tenants or from use received as a resident or business owner. Therefore in the vast majority of cases, historic preservation regulations and incentives not only allow but encourage a property owner to adaptively reuse a building in a fashion that provides utility in the marketplace.

**The Eli
New Haven, Connecticut**

Formerly the headquarters of Southern New England Telephone Company, now providing ground floor commercial space and luxury condominiums.

**The Wauregan
Norwich, Connecticut**

Built in 1855 as a hotel, the building now provides 70 units of affordable housing.

For historic buildings either to meet regulatory requirements or to receive incentives, the most significant character-defining features of a building will have to be maintained. Fortunately, the increase in the amount of adaptive reuse of historic buildings in the last 30 years has also caused a growth in expertise among architects, contractors, engineers and developers. Members of those professions have learned how to make design and construction decisions that not only preserve the historic character of the building but also add to the appeal of the structure to the marketplace, and to do so cost effectively.

Without a philosophy and practice of adaptive reuse in the United States the historic preservation movement would be far less successful.

Historic Preservation and Sustainable Development

In most of the world, *sustainable development* is seen as the "triple bottom line" approach to development – environmental responsibility, social responsibility and economic responsibility. There is increasing recognition that for a community to be viable there needs to be a link between environmental responsibility and economic responsibility; for a community to be livable there needs to be a link between environmental responsibility and social responsibility; and for a community to be equitable there needs to be a link between economic responsibility and social responsibility.

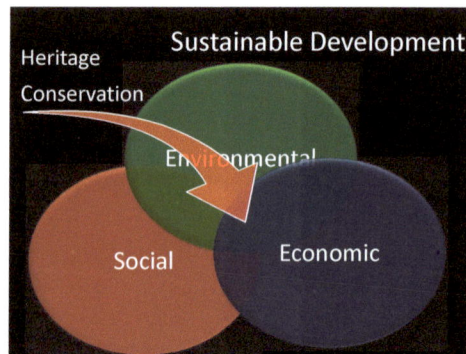

Dozens of activities can contribute to a comprehensive sustainable development strategy: energy conservation, clean water protection, preservation of farm land, reduced carbon emissions, etc. But the protection and reuse of heritage buildings is the only activity that is simultaneously meeting environmental responsibility, social responsibility and economic responsibility and that is simultaneously helping to make communities viable, livable and equitable.

The closest we have in America to a comprehensive sustainable development movement is known as *Smart Growth*. *Smart Growth* has a clear set of principles:

- Create a range of housing opportunities and choices

- Create walkable neighborhoods

- Encourage community and stakeholder collaboration

- Foster distinctive, attractive places with a Sense of Place

- Make development decisions predictable, fair, and cost effective

- Mix land uses

- Preserve open space, farmland, natural beauty and critical environmental areas

- Provide a variety of transportation choices

- Strengthen and direct development toward existing communities

- Take advantage of compact built design

Rural Pennsylvania

More American communities are recognizing that simply by preserving their historic commercial and residential neighborhoods, every one of the *Smart Growth* principles is advanced. Historic preservation *is* sustainable development.

The Tools of Historic Preservation

If the private sector is going to be expected to be responsible for most of the investment in historic buildings, then the tools to encourage that investment need to be provided. Governments at all three levels, and some non-profit and even for-profit entities, have developed not just tools, but entire tool boxes available for historic preservation. The following are some of the most frequently used ones.

Federal Rehabilitation Tax Credit

As has been noted, the federal government in the United States provides very few protections for historic properties. It does, however, provide incentives for the private sector to invest in heritage assets. Among the most successful incentive programs in the world for historic preservation is the Rehabilitation Tax Credit in the United States.

A *tax credit* is a dollar-for-dollar reduction in the amount that would otherwise have to be paid in taxes. If, for example, one had a tax liability of $15,000 but had a tax credit of $10,000, she would only have to remit $5,000 in taxes.

For owners and investors in historic properties, a tax credit is available to encourage redevelopment of heritage buildings. To receive the tax credit four tests must be met: 1) the property must be for investment or commercial use; 2) the amount of investment must be "substantial"[1]; 3) the property must be listed on the National Register of Historic Places or be eligible for listing; and 4) the work must be done consistent with the *Secretary's Standards for Rehabilitation*. If these tests are met, the investor receives a tax credit equal to 20% of the amount spent on rehabilitation. The qualifying expenditures do not have to be "historic." For example, an elevator might be installed into a building that never had an elevator. If that elevator is installed in such a fashion that the Secretary's Standards are met, 20 % of the cost of the elevator is a tax credit for the investor.

> **Example of the Federal Rehabilitation Tax Credit**
>
> Purchase Price of Property: $100,000
>
> Rehabilitation expenditure: $400,000.
>
> Tax credit received: $80,000 (20% of $400,000)
>
> Net cost to the owner after tax credit: $420,000 ($100,000 + $400,000 - $80,000)

State Tax Credits

More 30 states now have some form of tax credit for the rehabilitation of historic buildings. In most cases these can be used in addition to the federal credit. These state tax credits range from 5% to 25% of the rehabilitation expenditure. In the State of Oklahoma, for example, a project can receive a 20% tax credit against state tax liability in addition of the 20% credit against federal tax liability.

Furthermore, while the federal tax credit cannot be used for one's personal residence, most state tax credits can. Therefore individuals can buy a deteriorated historic house, rehabilitate it as their personal residence, and receive a tax credit for a portion of that expenditure.

> **Example of the Federal and State Rehabilitation Tax Credits**
>
> Purchase price of property: $100,000
>
> Rehabilitation expenditure: $400,000.
>
> Federal tax credit received: $80,000 (20% of $400,000)
>
> State tax credit received: $80,000 (20% of $400,000)
>
> Net cost to the owner after credits: $340,000 ($100,000 + $400,000 - $80,000 - $80,000)

---

1 "Substantial" in the tax code means the greater of $5,000 or the "basis of the building." "Basis of the building" is the purchase price less the amount attributable to land, less any accumulated depreciation, plus any capital improvements.

In nearly every case, as with the federal tax credit, the rehabilitation work has to be approved as being consistent with the Secretary's Standards for an owner to receive the credit.

Property Tax Incentives

Property taxes are used primarily by local governments to support schools and city services such as police and fire protection, water systems, local streets, etc. Property taxes are known as *ad valorum* taxes, in that they are based as a percentage of the value of the property being taxed. The amount on which the property tax is based is usually called the *assessed value*. While there are often complex formulas to determine the amount of taxes due, typically the annual property taxes in most parts of the United States would be between 1 ½ % and 2 ½ % of the value of the property. Thus a property worth, say, $100,000 could expect to be taxed at between $1,500 and $2,500 per year.

But this sometimes provides a disincentive to reinvest. For example, if a property is purchased for $100,000 but then $900,000 is spent in renovations, the assessed value may jump to $1,000,000 and the taxes to between $15,000 and $25,000 per year. Particularly in the early years after rehabilitation, the increased income that the building can generate may not be sufficient to pay that much in taxes.

To respond to this, 30 states have enacted some form of assessment freeze for the rehabilitation of historic buildings. In South Dakota, for example, in the above situation, the rehabilitated historic building will remain with an assessed value of $100,000 for five years after the rehabilitation is completed. This allows time for the property to get rented and an income stream established before the dramatic increase in property taxes has to be faced.

The number of years that the assessment freeze is in place varies from state to state but ranges between 3 and 15 years. Again, in most cases, in order for the owner to receive the assessment freeze the work would have to be done according to preservation design standards.

Low Interest Loans

In the end, historic buildings are still real estate. And real estate in the United States is an asset that typically is financed largely with borrowed money. Because of this, even a small change in the interest rate charged on the borrowed capital, or the time over which it is repaid, can have a dramatic impact on the viability of a potential real estate investment.

In recognition of this reality, and to encourage investment in historic buildings, low interest loans are often a useful tool for rehabilitation projects.

Madison, Indiana

In many Main Street communities, the local private sector banks will make a commitment to make loans at interest rates less than would otherwise be available, provided that the funds are used for rehabilitation of historic buildings in the downtown area and the work is done within preservation guidelines.

From the public sector, low interest loans are frequently provided by all three levels of government for projects that advance a public policy priority, such as low income housing, downtown revitalization or historic preservation.

Even the non-profit sector is occasionally the provider of low interest loans. A program has recently been announced by the

National Trust for Historic Preservation that commits $5 million in below-market-rate loans for affordable housing in older and historic neighborhoods. Non-profit development corporations, local governments and private sector developers are all eligible for these loans.

Grants

In the United States there are some programs that give direct grants to historic preservation projects. Mentioned earlier were the Preservation Services Fund Grants from the National Trust. Some statewide preservation groups such as Indiana Landmarks also have small grants.

At the federal government level there are not many specifically historic preservation grant funds for the "bricks and mortar" work of building rehabilitation. However other grant programs can often be used for historic preservation projects. One such source is Community Development Block Grants (CDBG) from the Department of Housing and Urban Development. Based on an allocation formula CDBG funds are given by HUD to local governments. Within limits, there is considerable flexibility in what the local governments can do with that money, and the rehabilitation of residential and non-residential properties is among the specifically authorized activities. This doesn't have to be used for historic buildings, but frequently is. CDBG monies are sometimes used by local governments on projects of their own but are often invested by local government into projects of the private or non-profit sectors.

State transportation departments receive a sizable portion of their funds from the federal government. In the past those moneys were often used exclusively to build highways. In recent years, however, federal law has required that state agencies spend at least 10% of their funds on "transportation enhancements." Various expenditures can qualify as "transportation enhancements" including bicycle paths, highway beautification, pedestrian bridges, etc. But investment in transportation-related historic facilities is also a specifically permitted expenditure. As a result dozens of historic train stations, bus depots and even private buildings facing state highways have received rehabilitation monies.

Nearly every state has some small grants program, often using funds received from the National Park Service. But a few states have sizable programs to assist historic preservation. Colorado is one of those.

In 1990 Colorado voters authorized casinos in three small historic towns in the Rocky Mountains – Central City, Black Hawk and Cripple Creek. Of the state's receipts from those casinos, 28% goes to the State Historical Fund. In the last 15 years some 3,300 projects have received funding that has totaled in excess of $200 million. Most of the money goes into acquisition and development of National Register properties. But also eligible for funding are educational programs, survey and planning activities, archaeological assessments, historic structure assessments, and emergency grants.

Other Tools

Income tax credits, property tax assessment freezes, low interest loans and grants are all widely used for historic preservation in the United States. But those are not the only tools. More complex incentives such as transferable development rights, preservation easement donations, tax increment financing, contingent loans and other incentives also may be available. Preservationist expertise, which at one time was limited to architectural styles and historic motifs, has now expanded to include an understanding of a wide range of sophisticated development tools to make historic preservation happen.

In those countries where most of the heritage conservation is done directly with public funds, such tools are probably less critical. But when the private sector and, to a lesser extent, the non-profit sector is expected to undertake most of the historic preservation activity, an array of useful tools is a key condition of widespread success.

Public-Private Partnerships and Historic Preservation

In both the United States and internationally, the public-private partnership (PPP) has gained favor as a means to tap the capital and the expertise of the private sector to advance public interests. PPPs have been developed and refined to meet a variety of needs, but the majority have arisen because of some combination of the following:

- There is a public need or a public benefit to be accrued through the arrangement.

- There is a need for private investment capital.

- There is a desire to leverage scarce public funds.

- There is an interest on the part of both the public and private sectors to share risks.

- The public sector lacks the development and/or management expertise to undertake the proposed project.

- There is a desire on the part of the public sector to enhance the value of an asset owned by it.

- The public sector wants to tap the innovation of the private sector.

- There is a need for ongoing public influence as to what happens to the public facility or service.

- There is a desire for a reversionary interest (i.e., ultimate return of the facility to public control) at some time in the future.

Most public-private partnerships have been for major infrastructure or facilities projects – airports, water treatment plants, toll roads, etc. But there is an emerging interest in using PPPs for historic buildings as well. Why? Because the reasons listed above for PPPs in general are also directly applicable to many historic buildings.

In the United States a number of federal agencies have entered into PPP agreements for historic property redevelopment including the National Park Service, the US Army and the General Services Administration. The following example of the Hotel Monaco in Washington, DC, is one of these success stories.

The principles and forms of transactions for PPPs are readily adaptable for historic building projects. There is one significant difference, however, between the large infrastructure PPP and one involving a heritage building: the non-profit sector is very likely to play a key role in the historic PPP. This may involve an ownership position in the final development or it may be serving as the proponent and watchdog over the project. But the natural grassroots constituency for historic buildings means, in the United States at least, that the NGO sector will often have a significant role to play.

A Closer Look: The General Services Administration and the Hotel Monaco

Washington, DC — The Old General Post Office was a problem. One of the oldest federal office buildings in the United States, it was built in phases between 1839 and 1866. It had been designated a National Historic Landmark on numerous grounds. Designed by the architect of the Washington Monument, this building had more than architectural significance. America's Pony Express was conceived there, and it was in this building where the first public telegraph office was located. In 1859 *Harper's Magazine* wrote, "We doubt there is a building in the world more chaste and architecturally perfect than the General Post Office."

But for over a decade the building in the heart of Washington, DC, stood empty. It was owned by the General Services Administration (GSA), the agency that serves as the "landlord" for the federal government, being responsible both for owning and managing government buildings and also finding privately owned space for other government departments. Repeated attempts to find a government entity to occupy the structure failed, with various agencies citing the building's configuration and rehabilitation cost as factors in declining to locate there.

Using a provision of the National Historic Preservation Act, the GSA released a request for proposals for the redevelopment of the General Post Office. Out of three responses, the selected proposal was a 184-room luxury hotel. This option was chosen because that use required the least change to the significant spaces of the building and also because of the ongoing public access a hotel would provide.

Main Players

The owner of the building and primary public partner is the GSA. Klimpton Hotel Group, a chain of small boutique hotels, is the private partner. Other government agencies are involved as well, however. The National Park Service is the primary federal department responsible for the stewardship of heritage buildings, and is also the entity that must approve projects to receive tax credits for the rehabilitation of historic properties. Other public agencies that had some review and approval role included the District of Columbia Historic Preservation Office, the Advisory Council on Historic Preservation and the Fine Arts Commission of Washington, DC.

The Transaction

The property was leased to the private partner for 60 years. The payment to the government is based on the financial success of the hotel operation, which is expected to be in excess of $50 million over the life of the lease. In addition the GSA invested $5 million in the construction costs, primarily for exterior restoration. The private partner's investment was approximately $40 million. In addition to earning operating revenues over the 60 years, the private partner received approximately $8 million in federal income tax credits which could be used as soon as the building was placed in service.

Historic Tax Credits

In the United States, federal tax law provides a tax incentive for the rehabilitation of historic buildings. An investor receives the tax credit if: 1) the property is designated as historic; 2) the property is income generating; and 3) the work done on the building meets the standards established for historic building renovation. If these tests are met, the investor receives a tax credit equal to 20% of the rehabilitation expenditure. A tax credit is a dollar-for-dollar reduction in income taxes payable. Thus a $40 million rehabilitation generated an $8 million tax credit.

Ordinarily it is only the owner who is entitled to a tax credit. But if there is a long-term tenant whose base lease is in excess of 39 years, the rehabilitation expenditure of that tenant qualifies for the tax credit as well. Thus it was essential to the transaction that the lease be longer than the 30 years the government originally favored since at that length of time no tax credits would have been available.

Benefits – Public Partner

The GSA was relieved of the obligation to maintain an empty historic building, will receive a distribution of revenues and will regain possession of the structure in habitable condition at the end of the lease period.

Benefits - Private Partner

In addition to the financial returns from operations and the approximately $8 million in credits against federal income tax liability, the hotel project has won numerous recognitions for its owners including several architectural design awards, five consecutive *Four Diamond* ratings from the American Automobile Association, and designations by *Conde Nast Traveler* as one of the 80 Top New Hotels in the World and one of the Top 700 Hotels in the World.

Local Government

While not a direct participant in the transaction, the government of the city of Washington also received measurable benefit. Under US law, properties owned by one level of the government are not taxable by another level of government. Thus the Hotel Monaco does not pay real property tax. However it is subject to bed tax, sales tax and income tax which will generate millions of dollars for the city government over the lifetime of the lease. In addition the hotel employs more than 75 workers.

Historic Preservation

This National Landmark has been restored to high standards and is accessible to the public, but has not been privatized by being sold off to a private owner.

Conclusion

Historic preservation in the United States is not about freezing the past or making cities passive museums. Not much of historic preservation in the United States is about mansions, museums or monuments, although all three have their place.

Mostly historic preservation in the United States is more about people than about buildings. It is about incorporating historic resources into the everyday lives of ordinary Americans.

In the United States the public sector provides protections and incentives. The non-profit sector provides education and advocacy. The private sector provides ownership and investment.

Historic preservation in the United States isn't a sentimental nostalgia for yesterday; it is about utilizing heritage resources today and investing in historic buildings for tomorrow.

America's towns, cities and neighborhoods are better places to live, work and play because of their historic buildings.

Historic preservation in America strengthens communities.

Appendix 1: To learn more about....

Source	Link
Advisory Council on Historic Preservation	http://www.achp.gov/
California Environmental Quality Act	http://ceres.ca.gov/ceqa/
Certified Local Governments	http://www.nps.gov/history/hps/clg/
Charleston's Old and Historic District	http://www.preservationsociety.org/program_process.asp
Colorado State Historical Fund	http://coloradohistory-oahp.org/programareas/shf/background.htm
Community Development Block Grants	http://www.hud.gov/offices/cpd/communitydevelopment/programs/
Downtown St. Louis Partnership	http://www.downtownstl.org/
Economic Development Administration Awards Program	http://www.eda.gov/ImageCache/EDAPublic/documents/pdf-docs/pdfdocs_202008/edaawardsbrochure2008_2epdf/v1/edaawardsbrochure2008.pdf
Executive Order 13006	http://www.gsa.gov/portal/content/100842
Executive Order 13287	http://www.preserveamerica.gov/EOtext.html
Federal Antiquities Act of 1906	http://www.nps.gov/archeology/sites/antiquities/about.htm
Federal Rehabilitation Tax Credit	http://www.nps.gov/history/hps/tps/tax/
Fire Station #7, West Hollywood, California	http://www.lahousingpartnership.com/Property_WestHollywood-FireHouse.html
General links to online preservation information	http://www.hpo.dcr.state.nc.us/links.htm
General Services Administration Historic Buildings Center	http://www.gsa.gov/portal/content/104441
HABS (Historic American Buildings Survey)	http://www.nps.gov/history/hdp/habs/index.htm\
Historic Preservation Commissions	http://www.uga.edu/napc/
HUD Secretary's Award for Excellence in Historic Preservation	http://www.huduser.org/research/secaward.html#hist
Indiana Landmarks	http://www.historiclandmarks.org/Pages/default.aspx
Midtown Exchange, Minneapolis	http://www.huduser.org/periodicals/Researchworks/june_07/RW_vol4num6t1.html
Mount Vernon Ladies' Association	http://www.mountvernon.org/
National Alliance of Preservation Commissions	http://www.uga.edu/napc/
National Center for Preservation Technology and Training	http://www.ncptt.nps.gov/
National Conference of State Historic Preservation Officers	http://www.ncshpo.org/
National Council for Preservation Education	http://www.uvm.edu/histpres/ncpe/
National Environmental Policy Act	http://www.epa.gov/Compliance/basics/nepa.html
National Heritage Areas	http://www.nps.gov/history/heritageareas/FAQ/INDEX.HTM
National Historic Preservation Act	http://www.nps.gov/history/local-law/FHPL_HistPrsrvt.pdf
National Main Street Center	http://www.mainstreet.org/
National Park Service – Cultural Resources	http://www.nps.gov/history/preservation.htm
National Preservation Institute	http://www.npi.org/

National Register of Historic Places	http://www.nps.gov/nr/about.htm
National Trust Community Investment Corporation	http://www.ntcicfunds.com/
National Trust Dozen Distinctive Destinations	http://www.preservationnation.org/travel-and-sites/travel/dozen-distinctive-destinations/
National Trust for Historic Preservation	http://www.preservationnation.org/
National Trust Most Endangered List	http://www.preservationnation.org/issues/11-most-endangered/
National Trust Preservation Books	http://www.preservationbooks.org/Bookstore.asp?Item=1107
National Trust Preservation Grants	http://www.preservationnation.org/resources/find-funding/nonprofit-public-funding.html
National Trust Rural Heritage Development Initiative	http://delta.preservearkansas.org/
Paducah, Kentucky Artist Relocation Program	http://www.paducaharts.com/
Pioneer Square Business Association	http://www.pioneersquare.org/
Preservation Action	http://www.preservationaction.org/
Preservation Briefs	http://www.nps.gov/history/hps/tps/briefs/presbhom.htm
Preservation Commission Design Guidelines	http://www.uga.edu/napc/programs/napc/guidelines.htm
Preservation Easements	http://www.preservationnation.org/resources/legal-resources/easements/
Preservation North Carolina	http://www.presnc.org/
Preservation North Carolina Easement Program	http://www.presnc.org/Property/Preservation-Easements
Preservation North Carolina Edenton Cotton Mill Village	http://www.presnc.org/Property/Edenton-Cotton-Mill-VillagePreservation Resource Center of New Orleans
Preserve America	http://www.preserveamerica.gov/
Savannah, Georgia Convention and Visitors Bureau	http://www.savannahvisit.com/
Save America's Treasures	http://www.saveamericastreasures.org/
Secretary's Standards	http://www.nps.gov/history/local-law/arch_stnds_8_2.htm
Section 106	http://www.achp.gov/106summary.html
Silver City, New Mexico Main Street Program	http://www.silvercitymainstreet.com/
Smart Growth Network	http://www.smartgrowth.org/about/default.asp
State Historic Preservation Offices	http://www.ncshpo.org/find/index.htm
State Tax Credit Programs	http://www.preservationnation.org/issues/rehabilitation-tax-credits/additional-resources/nthp_state_tax_credits_model_policy.pdf
The Arc	http://www.arcofthecapitalarea.org/index.php
Transportation Enhancement Funds	http://www.fhwa.dot.gov/environment/te/
US State Department Ambassador's Fund	http://exchanges.state.gov/culprop/afcp/info.htm
US/ICOMOS	http://www.usicomos.org/
Vieux Carré Commission	http://www.nola.gov/en/RESIDENTS/Vieux-Carre-Commission/

Appendix 2: The Secretary's Standards for Rehabilitation

1. A property shall be used for its historic purpose or be placed in a new use that requires minimal change to the defining characteristics of the building and its site and environment.

2. The historic character of a property shall be retained and preserved. The removal of historic materials or alteration of features and spaces that characterize a property shall be avoided.

3. Each property shall be recognized as a physical record of its time, place, and use. Changes that create a false sense of historical development, such as adding conjectural features or architectural elements from other buildings, shall not be undertaken.

4. Most properties change over time; those changes that have acquired historic significance in their own right shall be retained and preserved.

5. Distinctive features, finishes, and construction techniques or examples of craftsmanship that characterize a historic property shall be preserved.

6. Deteriorated historic features shall be repaired rather than replaced. Where the severity of deterioration requires replacement of a distinctive feature, the new feature shall match the old in design, color, texture, and other visual qualities and, where possible, materials. Replacement of missing features shall be substantiated by documentary, physical, or pictorial evidence.

7. Chemical or physical treatments, such as sandblasting, that cause damage to historic materials shall not be used. The surface cleaning of structures, if appropriate, shall be undertaken using the gentlest means possible.

8. Significant archeological resources affected by a project shall be protected and preserved. If such resources must be disturbed, mitigation measures shall be undertaken.

9. New additions, exterior alterations, or related new construction shall not destroy historic materials that characterize the property. The new work shall be differentiated from the old and shall be compatible with the massing, size, scale, and architectural features to protect the historic integrity of the property and its environment.

10. New additions and adjacent or related new construction shall be undertaken in such a manner that if removed in the future, the essential form and integrity of the historic property and its environment would be unimpaired.

www.ingramcontent.com/pod-product-compliance
Lightning Source LLC
Chambersburg PA
CBHW041548040426
42447CB00002B/87